Where There's Tea There's Hope

T G Carter

Windmill Hill Publishing

Also by Trevor G Carter:
Diamonds in the Desert
Children of the Fire
Taking Stock

All Rights Reserved

ISBN 978-0-9557426-3-7

First published 2015 by
Windmill Hill Publishing

Printed in Great Britain by
Printondemand-worldwide

Contents

Food for Thought

On the Dark Side

Singalong Songs

Introduction

On the Light Side: If you are in search of the light you will be hard pressed not to find pointers in these pages. Take pity on the afflicted as you empathise with the trials and tribulations of 'Frank N Stein', learn vital tips on how to deal with 'Blue Mondays', revel in the sensuality of 'Love in the Morning'. If that doesn't make you feel better then rejoice in the timeless truth of 'Where There's Tea, There's Hope!'.

Views on News: The news is a constant source of poetic provocation. Delve into the educational controversy of 'Head Talk', studiously deliberate on whether to judge the non-judgmental vicar, take an unflinching look at the ugly side of nakedness and consider the pros and cons of Britannia's possible divorce. Yes, there's much to chew on, think about and talk about. You can exchange views on these crucial issues and use them to sow discord with friends and family.

Food for Thought: Have you had enough sex? If not, does it really matter? Are you your brother's keeper, and if you aren't should you be? Who should we feel most sorry for? What is it that really matters? You'll find explorations of these deep and meaningful questions here. Deep and yet oddly accessible.

On the Dark Side: Saddle up and ride with the Horsemen of the Apocalypse into a world of Blakeian dystopia wherein you can consider whether my land really is your land, survey divided paths and poignant reunions and worry whether those who've led us in are able to lead us out.

Singalong Songs: Join in the rousing choruses that pithily express our popular sentiments. Confirm your powerlessness by means of a futile gesture as you sing along to 'Super Callous Banking Bastards'.

On the Light Side

We Are Very Lucky (to all brave spirits)

We are very lucky, you and I.
We know the things we have to do.
We look life firmly in the eye.

Not all folks live before they die;
they don't resist the tyrant's screw.
They are not brave like you and I.

And as their passage here flies by
they do what others tell them to.
They do not look life in the eye.

Acceptance is their alibi;
a crumbling crutch to help them through.
They are not brave like you and I.

Let's pity those who do not try
to honour all that they can do.
They do not look life in the eye.

They suppress their alter ego's cry
to strive for what is right and true.
Still, we are lucky, you and I.
We look life firmly in the eye.

Book Launch at a Lakeland Show

Poetry books are launched at elegant soirées
accompanied by dry white wine.
Poetry books are launched at literary lunches
with tables where authors sign…but not mine, not mine.
You see, I'd called my northern agent
to discuss my book launch plan.
I said, I need some gigs in Lakeland.
I said, just do what you can.

She came back with some fixtures.
One was called the Loweswater Show.
I thought, well, okay, fair enough.
But little did I know
that this show had entertainments
so bizarre and so diverse
that I just had to write about them.
And that's the subject of this verse.

I wasn't sure how to react as
I was a stranger in that land.
So I strolled around the tractors
looking for a place to stand.
Then I asked a passing steward -
'Please, where's the poetry tent?'
He said, 'Oh poh-tree, tis over there'.
And thus directed, off I went…

but found the tent was labelled 'POULTRY'!
This generated deep self-doubt.
And though I felt sad and lonely,
I didn't chicken out.

I'd never read poems in a poultry tent.
It seemed an odd sort of idea.
But as I was only being paid a paltry sum
I thought, well, what's there to fear?

I took an interest in the rams,
the pride of local flocks;
while the farmers in the poultry tent
displayed their finest cocks.
I mingled with the surging crowds,
the heaving rustic masses.
I joined in all their country games,
their esoteric classes…

Ram with the best teeth
Farmer with the best teeth
Quickest dog when owner calls
Smartest bull with biggest horns
Best calf on a halter led by child under ten
The most handsome pig since…I don't know when
The best matching jumpers on a ewe and her lamb
The most tantalising texture in a blackcurrant jam
An owner and animal that look most alike
Best animal impersonation at the open mic
The most handsome farmer
The least alarmed llama
Best blue cheese
Best blue joke
Best beer belly on big fat bloke
    …and so the list went on.

And yet I romped home in my class…
the only poet they could get.
And I still have the red rosette,
the strangest prize that I've won yet.
It was a gig I will always remember:
the first poet of the Loweswater Show!
I'm going back there next September.
My northern agent's fun to know.

Love in the Morning

Be there for me each morning
to help me start the day,
though I can't give you a warning
when I have to have my way.

I need to know your body
awaits me when I wake
to help to keep me going.
Be there, for my heart's sake.

I'll drizzle you with honey,
I'll take you deep inside.
And I don't need much money
to claim you as my bride.

Be there for me forever
to fuel my inner glow.
Oh Porridge, how I love you.
I had to let you know.

Wi-fi Wife

He introduced himself as Virgin,
(though he looked the worldly type).
Mr V was selling Wi-fis
and I fell for his hype.

My marriage was in tatters,
I was in an awful state,
and Mr V said he could fix me up
at a buy-now-discount-rate.

When I confessed my wife was leaving
he said 'Look, these Wi-fis are much better!
So don't waste your time in grieving.
If she wants to go, then let her.

You're never alone with a Wi-fi
and a Wi-fi can be trusted.'
So I signed up for a Wi-fi trial.
I felt confused and flustered.

I said 'Tell me more about the Wi-fi.
How do men…turn them on?'
He said 'Oh, nothing could be simpler.
This answer won't take long.

You just make up a password
then type it on a screen.'
I said 'I'm no good at making passes.
Will she know what I mean?'

He said 'Oh yes, no problem.
A Wi-fi has a simple heart.'
And though I felt a bit suspicious
I agreed that I'd take part.

Well, it sounded too good to be true,
but I thought…hmm, give it a try.
My wife had clearly had enough,
so why not try Wi-fi?

We got along quite well at first.
We 'connected' every day.
She seemed to come quite quickly.
She didn't need foreplay.

She never once refused me.
She responded to each touch.
Well, I soon forgot about my wife;
and Wi-fis don't cost much.

But then, a few weeks later,
I unveiled her fatal flaw
when I found out that my Wi-fi
had served the bloke next door.

My Wi-fi'd been unfaithful!
Now what is a man to do
when his Wi-fi puts herself about
and serves the neighbours too?

And it wasn't just a one-off!
It wasn't just a little fling.
I suppose I am old-fashioned
but I can't bear that sort of thing.

No, it wasn't just a quickie.
They'd been doing it for weeks.
And I only got to find out
when I looked on WikiLeaks!

So I called up Mr Virgin
and said 'What have you got to say?'
But Mr V was unrepentant.
He said 'They make Wi-fis that way.'

I felt abused and disillusioned.
But had I been a tad naïve
to put my faith in a new Wi-fi
who was programmed to deceive?

Well, by that time I had had enough.
I've given up my Wi-fi life.
I like to know what's mine is mine.
I need a proper wife.

The Love Life of the Collared Dove

Thoughts on watching a collared dove on a hotel roof garden.

Around the hotel garden
pecks the collared dove.
She never stops to think about
what she wants from love.

The hotel guests bask thoughtfully,
penned by the tasteful fence,
all mindful of how human love
is cloaked in thin pretence.

And aware of their impurities,
the couples cling in pairs;
all masking insecurities,
some dreaming of affairs.

For deep within each human heart
there lie those secret vaults
which a holiday can excavate
to display long hidden faults.

Oh, if all human hearts could soar
as freely as the birds,
there would be no need any more
for love besmirched by words.

Frank N Stein: in his own words

'Frankenstein' was written by Mary Shelley and published in 1818. In Shelley's story, Victor Frankenstein was the creator of the monster. In the stage adaptation by Peggy Webling, the monster was named Frankenstein after its creator. In this account, the monster describes his feelings about being himself.

My name is Frank, Frank N Stein.
Though my reputation is malign
I cannot help the way I am.
I am *not* an ordinary man.

To be quite frank, I am a freak.
I'm known for my sadistic streak,
as I'm unpleasant, grim and scary.
If you want trouble, go on, dare me!

I sleep all day, come out at night.
I do not care much for the light,
as in the light it's plain to see
everything that's wrong with me.

Yes, I've got problems, born this way.
I was designed to spread dismay.
I'm the sort of dude that people diss.
Blame Shelley, she made me like this.

But honestly, it is no joke
being such a sad repulsive bloke.
To be frank, I'd rather be benign;
but I can't, because I'm Frank N Stein.

It is a very lonely life –
no chance of getting a normal wife.
So I went back to meet my maker,
said 'I need a wife. Could you generate her?

After all, you have created me!'
She said 'Well, I'm not sure. I'll have to see.
It would be hard to make a mate for you.'
I said 'I'm not fussy. Anything will do.'

She said 'Yes, but Frank, remember this:
you're not the sort of bloke girls like to kiss.
So I'll have to make her quite like you.'
I said 'Okay! Okay! Anything will do!'

Go on, ask me what the N stands for…
it stands for Norman!
Normal Norman? What a joke.
You can see I'm *not* a normal bloke!

I've got this bolt screwed through my neck.
I'm full of problems. I'm a wreck!
Normal Norman? That's a laugh!
I'm crazy! I'm a psychopath!

I've got no sisters, friends or brothers.
I get my kicks by scaring others!
Though as I've said, I'd rather be benign;
but I can't because I'm Frank N Stein.

Looking at me, you may think it odd
that I'm tired of being on my tod.
People say 'Ooh, that Frank!
He always tries to scare me!'

The normal people just can't bear me!
Wherever I go, they won't let me in.
They take one look and scream
'Oh no! Not him!'

And the thing that really, really bugs me
is when girls say 'Frank, you are so ugly
that I would rather tramp to Timbuktu
than go out on a date with you.'

Still, I'm used to these depressing scenes.
Go on, ask me what the 'Stein' bit means...
it stands for stone.
And because I'm not normal flesh and bone
I'm doomed to live my life alone.

I know my presence will offend.
There's no one I can call a friend.
I want a woman to call mine.
I can't get one 'cos I'm Frank N Stein.

I've been for therapy – didn't help.
The psychiatrist let out a yelp
and said 'Oh no, I can't help you.
You've got problems that I can't unscrew.

Quite frankly Frank, you are revolting.
And whoever put that massive bolt in
to your neck must have been mad.
No, there is no hope for you, my lad.'

I realised that he was right.
And that's why I avoid the light.
And that's why horror is my line.
I have been frank. I'm Frank N Stein.

In Search of the Light

'Have you got a light?' asked the sad young man
in a pleading, hopeful tone.
I was quick with reassurance,
for no man should walk alone.

'Oh yes, oh yes; I have a light!
Oh yes, indeed I do.
Let me guide you through the darkness.
Let me share my light with you.

Behold the thoughts of Socrates
and the wisdom of Gibran.
Study the great philosophers,
then you'll be Enlightened Man!

Then you won't be approaching strangers
asking them to point the way.
For once you find your own true path
you'll have no need to stray.'

Then quizzically, he stared at me
and said 'Hey man, is this a joke?
I'm only asking for a light.
I guess that you don't smoke.'

I said 'Oh no, I don't need smoke.
That's not what I desire,
for I am fuelled by an inner light
that sets my world on fire.'

And then he upped and walked away,
for my words failed to ignite
the imagination of that dude
who'd asked me for a light.

Blue Monday

This was written at Radio Bristol as an on-air challenge to help Bristolians cope with going back to work after Christmas. I was asked by a positive psychologist, who was also a guest on the programme, to include the words 'cold turkey', 'interaction' and 'achievement'.

I've been asked to turn Blue Monday red
to help you all get out of bed
and say goodbye to Monday blues
and look on Mondays as good news.

Get out! Get going! Get in the pink
and find that magic Monday link.
As Monday starts each week anew
there ain't no point in feeling blue.

Identify a new achievement!
Let go the blues, forget bereavement.
Now that the turkey's old and cold
this is the season to be bold.

Go out and find some interaction -
that is the route to satisfaction.
Blue Mondays? It need not be so!
And if you're looking for somewhere to go

then why not book a cabaret?
Get therapy for your dismay!
Music, magic and circus fun
will get your blue notes on the run.

To find out details, if you will,
just google Bard of Windmill Hill.
Be sure to get your tickets booked -
and once you've been, then you'll be hooked.

Where There's Tea, There's Hope!

This phrase is attributed to Sir Arthur Wing Pinero, a 19th century playwright.

I was feeling sad and weary,
dispirited and flat,
when a message beckoned to me...
and I thought, right, I'm buying that!

I was on a shopping mission.
I was struggling to cope.
And then I spied a card that read
'Where there's tea, there's hope'.

I felt I had to buy it
to remind us that it's true.
These words have meant a lot to me
and I hope they will to you.

For I like pearls of wisdom.
Fine words can float my boat.
So I wrote this to celebrate
'Where there's tea, there's hope'.

Who needs psychotherapy
when a card can do the trick?
And if I had to choose one card
this is the card I'd pick.

As when one's getting older,
on the downside of the slope;
the thought it bears is cheering:
'Where there's tea, there's hope'.

Some sayings are cathartic;
they go straight to your heart.
And when we need to stop and think
they nudge us all to start.

It's the verbal panacea,
the all-purpose antidote;
it's echoed down the ages:
'Where there's tea, there's hope'.

Who needs fancy cocktails,
designer drugs or dope
when you can put the kettle on
saying 'Where there's tea, there's hope'?

Almost everybody likes it;
even a misanthrope.
Its ubiquity just serves as proof
that 'Where there's tea, there's hope'.

The Tommies in the trenches –
what did they want the most?
Did they long for porridge?
Did they long for toast?

Did they lust for women?
No! Historians all agree
the thing the Tommies wanted most
was just a cup of tea.

The Chinese invented many things:
gunpowder; paper; clocks.
But there's another, more important one;
an absorber for life's shocks.

You know the thing I'm thinking of.
I've mentioned it before.
It's the thing the Tommies wanted most
when they were in the war.

It's the international lubricant;
ask Obama or the Pope.
They will not dispute the fact
that 'Where there's tea, there's hope'.

Now everything that we take in
affects the way we think.
The sort of people we become
depends on what we drink.

Coffee messes with your head.
It's worse than LSD!
Do not indulge in coffee.
It's best to stick to tea.

Strong liquor drives you crazy.
Beer makes you weak and fat.
Drinking wine can make you lazy.
Well…what's the point of all of that?

All alternatives are inferior.
Now I feel I've made my case
for the drink that is superior,
for the drink we can't replace.

Comrades! Brothers! Sisters!
Come fill your hearts with glee!
For you can never be alone in life
so long as you have tea.

It's the universal beverage.
Come on now, have a vote.
Raise your hand if you believe
that 'Where there's tea there's hope'.

For where there's tea there's joyfulness.
So don't sit around and mope.
Go, reach out for your teapot
saying 'Where there's tea, there's hope'.

Behold the potent saying
and the power it can contain.
It can dissolve depression
if it infiltrates your brain.

So if you're sad and lonely
and you need an antidote,
just recall these words of comfort:
'Where there's tea, there's hope'.

Imbibe this incantation!
We've learnt it now by rote.
Let all the world proclaim it:
'Where there's tea, there's hope'!

The wisdom of the ancient Greeks
could not strike a higher note.
Say it, chant it, shout it:
'Where there's tea, there's hope'!

When life gets overwhelming,
when you need a bit more rope;
when it gets as bad as it can get,
think 'Where there's tea, there's hope'.

Views on News

Guns for the Blind

An article in Private Eye highlighted that in Iowa there are no restrictions on blind people acquiring a firearms licence. A spokesperson for the Iowan authorities justified the policy as follows:

Oh holy smoke! Oh golly gee!
Let's see how wild the West can be!
We'll show the world defiantly
this land is well and truly free.

An to prove we are the carin kind
we're givin guns out to the blind.
You wanna gun, then take one mate.
We ain't folks who discriminate!

Heck, we don't mind if you can't see.
This land was made for you an me.
So sign up old son, just make your mark,
then take your shotgun to the park…

point your weapon - who knows where?
In Iowa there's guns to spare.
Go shoot at anythin at all.
Get trigger happy, have a ball.

Guns for the blind? It makes good sense.
Why should the blind have no defence?
And anyways, remember this:
blind folks'll very likely miss.

So they can help to scare the hoods
without much chance of spillin blood.
No, we don't care for gun restrictions.
They don't fit with our predilections.

So don't bring us no condemnation.
We'll blow away intimidation!
Our message here is loud and clear:
in Iowa, don't interfere!

This land was built by cowboys who
believed in violence through an through.
So hereabouts we are inclined
to give out guns to folks who're blind.
Yes siree!

Punchbag Pope

In January 2015 the Pope said that in some circumstances he could understand people reacting violently to verbal abuse and that if anyone insulted his mother he would be inclined to give them a punch.

The good book says 'an eye for an eye',
so if you mess with me, be prepared to die.
I'll slap one cheek, then I'll slap another:
Rule One in life – defend your mother!

Free speech? Well, okay, to a point.
But your face could end up out of joint
if you insult my dear old mum.
If you don't like her, then just stay schtum.

Hey, I'm your modern punchbag Pope.
You feel oppressed? I'll bring you hope.
Forget that stuff about being meek.
The Lord does NOT admire the weak.

So defend yourself and learn to box.
Hit back when life deals out its knocks.
The Lord helps those who help each other.
Rule One in life – defend your mother!

Recall your history, all those wars?
God will defend a righteous cause.
And when right's not clear and he can't decide...
you'll find him fighting on both sides.

Yes, the good book's full of death and glory;
the Old Testament's especially gory.
So remember, if you are attacked:
God blesses those who can hit back.

Crusades and conquests, he was there;
helping Christians take the lion's share.
For those who aren't sure what is right;
the best response is…smite, smite, smite!

Don't get me wrong. Don't pick a fight.
But if you're picked on…then it's alright.
Insults can hurt you more than stones.
I know that's true deep in my bones.

So, smite those who dare insult your mother.
And smite those who have not discovered
that the word of God is always right.
When doubt arises…smite, smite, smite!

Expert Advice

I was bemused by this NHS advertising poster: 'If you are over sixty and feeling under the weather then consult your doctor or pharmacist.'

Beware you sexagenarians!
It's dangerous being old.
You should all see your doctor
and do what you are told.

Whatever there is wrong with you
some pills will do the trick.
So go and see your doctor.
Get diagnosed as sick.

If you woke up with a headache,
who knows what that may mean?
Go get some medication
to wipe your memory clean.

And if you're feeling sad and miserable,
then you're probably depressed.
So you should see your doctor,
as doctors know what's best.

And if you're plagued by aches and pains;
we beg you, don't delay.
You never know what they may mean.
See your doctor right away.

Better still, call an ambulance!
Go on, dial nine nine nine.
Tell them that you're sixty.
Sixty's a fatal sign!

They'll whisk you in for surgery
and check out your worn out parts.
They're bound to find that *something's* wrong.
Stop disease before it starts!

They'll fiddle with your tired bits
that have served you for too long.
You shouldn't ask too much of them.
They never were that strong.

So beware you sexagenarians.
It's dangerous being old.
It's time to call your doctor
and do what you are told.

They've drugs for every ailment,
there's lots from which to pick.
It's time to see your doctor
and get diagnosed as sick.

They have pills to make you younger.
They have pills to cheer you up.
Modern medicine's a wonder.
Drink from the magic cup.

Don't worry about the side effects.
They've got pills for that too!
Put your faith in experts.
Let them be the death of you.

Serco

'Without Serco, Britain would struggle to go to war.'
The Daily Telegraph

We once had a public service.
It was owned by you and me.
It looked after and preserved us
to help us be all we can be.
It was not designed for profit.
It was designed for public good.
Now everything is changing.
We're not standing where we stood.

Serco's in the service business;
and it's servicing itself.
It's taking over services
to inflate its private wealth.
It is big and it is greedy
and it's almost everywhere,
making money from the needy
while it pretends to care.

When I was recently inspected
at my job in education,
an aspect I'd not expected
was sustaining this creation.
The observation of my teaching
had a worrying connection
as Serco sucked a profit from
my compulsory inspection.

The defence of our great nation –
who d'you think controls the system?

I suppose when Serco got there
the ministry could not resist them.
You could say it's omnipresent,
and I find that ominous.
This feeling is unpleasant.
I'm inclined to make a fuss.

And in our grimmest institutions
where the ne'er-do-wells all dwell
Serco's locked into a contract
to ensure they're there as well,
correcting all the criminals
and protecting us from them:
the omnipresent organiser
has it sorted yet again.

Now though Serco isn't bragging
it sure has a lot of neck.
It also offers tagging
to keep criminals in check.
This is a handy earner
that Serco could not resist
and to boost its profit margin
they tag some who don't exist.

Now I must end this lamentation
before we get depressed
by this dreadful situation.
But should this poem be assessed?
And if so, who will do it?
Who would like to have a go?
I could send it off to Serco.
They're the people who should know.

Charlie's Lament: how long must one keep holding on?

I've just been watching the TV news.
It's only served to feed my blues.
It's time I had a proper job
and it's my birthright to be top nob.

Yes, she's been splendid; but, you know,
I do think Mummy ought to go.
Why must she keep on hanging on?
Why won't she pass the crown to one?

Now, I think it's time I wrote to her
suggesting that she should defer
and pass the top job on to one.
It's really time that she was gone.

So let's get started right away…
hmm, where to begin? What can one say?
I must be kind, yet clear and strong
to convince her that she should be gone.

'Dear Mummy, listen; hear my plea.
It's your son, Charlie. Yes, it's me.
Now, I know you've had a splendid reign
but listen to this news from Spain!

Well…King Juan Carlos, I've been told,
has brought his son in from the cold.
He's deemed it right to end his reign.
Oh Mummy; *do* please do the same.

Look, we really can't go on like this.
Quite frankly Mummy, it takes the piss
to keep one waiting for so long.
Oh, Mummy, Mummy, please be gone.

One has been waiting all one's life.
One even took that odd first wife
to impress the world and look the part.
Oh, come on Mummy. Let me start!

Come on now, Mummy, take a hint.
You've really overdone your stint.
It's only fair. Why *can't* you see
you should give your bloody job to me?

It's most unseemly at your age
the way you *cling on* to the stage.
So Mummy, Mummy, please be gone
and do pass on the crown to one.

Yes, I know some have suggested that
I wouldn't look good in your hat
and it should go straight to my boy!
But don't do that! That would destroy

the things we're here to represent.
For after all, who could invent
a system so beloved as ours
where we, the royals, hang on to powers

that lesser nations have dismissed.
Don't *do* that Mummy! Oh *do* resist!
If you think it through you *must* agree
the crown should come direct to *me*.

You know we are both getting on.
It's my turn now. I haven't long.
It's time you wrote down your swansong.
Oh, don't keep going on and on!

It's unbecoming. It's all wrong.
For God's sake hit that final gong.
Oh, Mummy, Mummy, *please* be gone.
It's time to pass the crown to one!'

Prince George is One

Proclaim it from the rooftops!
Good Prince George is one!
He's celebrating his first birthday.
It's a right royal carry on.
It's been in all the papers.
It's been on the telly too.
Prince George enjoys his capers –
one does what one must do.
He knows he's really special.
You can tell he's very bright –
just like all his family.
How he fills us with delight!
So proclaim it from the rooftops!
Good Prince George is one!
He's celebrating his first birthday.
It's a right royal carry on.

In Gaza kids are slaughtered –
in Syria and Iraq.
Once peace has been abandoned
they'll stage their next attack.
In Nigeria girls are rounded up
by nutters dressed in black
to serve demented warlords.
Many captives don't come back.
And there are many poor children
in England's pleasant land.
They are members of the underclass
who don't quite understand
the way the world is ordered
and how the system's set
for the rich to be rewarded
and for them to live in debt.

It's better that the taxes
support the true blue blood.
It's such a pity, all that poverty.
We'd help them if we could.
But the world is full of problems.
It ever has been thus.
So let us celebrate Prince George
and not make too much fuss.
Proclaim it from the rooftops!
Good Prince George is one!
He's celebrating his first birthday.
It's a right royal carry on.
Prince George is so delightful,
he's full of funny tricks.

And quite unlike his grandad,
he abstains from politics.
He's such a natural charmer.
He's destined for success.
He could be the next Obama
according to the press.

The media is a circus.
It keeps us in the dark.
They design it to divert us.
It's been so since the ark.
We know what gets reported
but not what gets ignored.
We'll never get it sorted.
The news is always flawed.

Enjoy your birthday, Georgie.
You're not the one to blame.
One does the things one has to.
The rules remain the same.

Britannia Considers Divorce

In 2014 Britannia started to think,
perhaps the time has come to break the link?
I know our marriage is deeply rooted
but Old Jock and I were never really suited.
Perhaps we've been together for too long?
After three hundred years things can go wrong.

The kids have left, got independence.
So what's our role? We've got no reference.
He's always been more left-wing than me.
Maybe the time is right to set him free?
But will he be safe in the world alone?
He's a bit naïve. It's widely known.

Down the centuries, he was quite loyal;
until he got drunk on North Sea oil.
That black gold went straight to his head -
made him turn a deeper shade of red.
Then he started to go cold on me
when he fell for that tart, the SNP;
drinking all night with his 'tartan army'.
Most of them are completely barmy!

For example, I think he's lost his senses
when it comes to thinking about defences.
He talks about demilitarisation.
That's not the talk of a grown-up nation.
And what of the cost? We can't afford a
reconstruction of that ancient border.
After all, who was it who turned the globe half pink?
Me and Old Jock. It makes you think.

Still…I suppose nothing goes on forever.
And I've got lots of memories to treasure.
We fought side by side. We've survived a lot.
Is our marriage worth a final shot?
Or should I say to Old Jock, 'Look, depart in peace'
- for love isn't love that can't release.

Thou Shalt not Judge: a judgement on the Reverend Tomlinson and the funeral of Ronnie Biggs

I wrote this in response to the funeral of the 'great' train robber Ronnie Biggs. The Great Train Robbery (1963) is one of Britain's most notorious crimes.

The Bible says we should not judge.
On this, the vicar will not budge
as he bids goodbye to Ronnie Biggs.
This vicar likes to get the gigs
that other vicars tend to shun
as he blesses lives spent on the run.
Though not all Christians agree
that blessings should be quite so free.

This vicar says we should love each other
and that we should not judge our brother.
He says that there's both bad and good
contained in everybody's blood.
And he points out Jesus thought the same,
hanging out with women on the game
and ne'er-do-wells of varied sorts,
according to first hand reports.

Yet it strikes me as a trifle mad
to imply that Biggs was *not that bad*.
I contend that judging's in our blood
along with all that bad and good.
So it's odd to be all hunky-dory
when recollecting Biggs's story.
Before absolution can begin
should we not at least confess some sin?

But Ronnie Biggs did not repent.
He seemed quite happy to be bent.
Although everyone's both bad and good;
well, most of us are mostly good.
And we would condemn Biggs's bad act.
Though that's a judgement, not a fact.
So now it seems that I have judged
the reverend who refused to judge.

I don't know if you'd judge him too.
I'll leave that judgement up to you.
Look, I'm not the retributive kind.
I know an eye for an eye makes the whole world blind,
but there's something here that's not quite right.
We should say our goodbyes in the light
and admit to what has gone before.
We can't bury truth behind death's door.

Head Talk

News item: 'Head teacher spends £50,000 on a one day training course organised by his friend.'

Hi! I'm your new head teacher.
My style is rather flash.
I am a modern creature;
a tad rash with your cash.

It's only public money.
It's there for me to use.
I try to spend it wisely.
Oh, I do hope you'll excuse

that fifty grand on training,
but it was a fun filled day.
My mate had organised it.
I trust that that's okay?

The governors are pesky;
thought best they didn't know.
They'd pose a load of questions;
daft bureaucracy you know.

I prefer the tsar based system –
make bosses free to choose.
There's rules, but we can twist 'em.
What have we got to lose?

Testing, testing, testing.
Strive towards the light!
We can always shift the goalposts
further to the right.

38

The unions are angry;
but then, they always are:
objected to my pay rise
and my new Jaguar.

They whinge about the hours.
They say that they're too much.
But I've got all the power
and they're all out of touch.

Academies! I love 'em!
The best thing since sliced bread.
You can have a lot of fun here
if you've been made THE HEAD.

Charlies

The world is full of charlies
who proclaim 'Je suis', 'Je suis'.
But Erdogan and Putin
are not fooling me.

Do they think they can be Charlies
through fatuous incantation?
These charlies are just charlies
who exploit the situation.

If you want to be a Charlie
then put your own head on the block.
For the legions of pretenders,
Charlie Hebdo's right to mock.

Centre Ground

Suffocating on the centre ground
they beam out their perfected smiles.
They are our modern politicians
preparing for the media trials.

As none may dare to speak their minds
they select safe words that all portray
the safety of their party lines;
red, blue and yellow…masked with grey.

Most feel the only safe position
is to try to sound just like the rest,
as they denounce the lies of the opposition
and state how they will be the best.

Proclaim the politics of 'one nation'
for hard-working folk of every class!
But keep a lid on imagination
or who knows what may come to pass?

The impulsive tweet or careless reference
could spell the end of their career.
So they tread lightly with tact and deference
telling punters what they want to hear.

And wary of the mighty media,
they cling tight to their party's plan,
haunted by the ghost of Emily Thornberry
and her fatal crash with White Van Man.

Politics as career, not conviction,
is how the party game is played,
resulting in spiritual dereliction
and the sadness of ideals betrayed.

Power, like wealth, always trickles upwards.
Fortune favours those who most conform;
who go with the flow, avoid corruption
and emulate the grey suit norm.

Ideology? Don't say that word!
Don't talk of values and ideas.
It's best to keep your message blurred.
Trade less on hopes and more on fears.

The Cloak of Nakedness

Nakedness is everywhere –
the unclad body sells.
Celebrities appear bare
to cast seductive spells
that get us all to part with cash,
so we'll be successful too
by splashing out and being rash.
It's the modern way to woo.

Yes, everything is hanging out
on unashamed display.
The celebs all put themselves about
to make the punter pay
for fancy clothes and flashy cars
that define the word 'success',
so the young will ogle at the stars
and aspire to their excess.

Beware the stuff they advertise
to the innocence of youth.
Beware the forms of nakedness
that cover up the truth.

'We've Decided to Consciously Uncouple'

As announced by Gwyneth Paltrow and Chris Martin in March 2014.

'We've decided to uncouple' -
it's celebrity divorce
celebrating its own language
when love has run its course…
they do not speak of splitting up –
no, no, that sounds too blunt.
They gaze into love's empty cup
and put on a cheerful front.

'We will consciously uncouple.'
'We will copulate no more.'
'No longer shall we masquerade
and hide our union's flaw.'
'We're really still the best of friends
and we'll co-parent from afar.'
'It's gone too far to make amends,
our love's a tarnished star.'
'So we'll consciously uncouple,
become legally unhitched.'
'The deal's not worth the trouble.'
'Our contract has been ditched.'
'It's a cognitive detachment.'
'It's a parting of the ways.'
'We're letting go of our attachment.'
'We've established separate caves.'
'This statement is our swan song.'
'We no longer are as one.'
'It's not that we are splitting up,
the circus will go on.'

Goodbye Bob: an elegy for Bob Crow (1961 – 2014)

'In life, you never get what you deserve: you get what you negotiate.'
The Accidental Apprentice, Vikas Swarup

The union movement sighs 'Oh no.
Bob was much too young to go.'
He was committed, staunch and true.
And now he's gone, aged fifty-two.

Vilified by Murdoch's press
for the power they could not suppress.
A grand a week to drive a train!
He drove rail management insane
as he held the RMT aloft
and claimed the communists were too soft.
He took no prisoners, shot from the hip,
was famous for his iron grip.

The product of a bolder age,
he fought to raise his workers' wage.
A tough guy and a cheeky geezer;
he stood his ground, was no appeaser.

Though Bob has gone to rest in peace
the workers' struggle does not cease.
And as the bankers steal our hard-earned pay
we cast around in disarray;
while maybe, from a perch on high,
in a workers' heaven in the sky,
Bob will whisper 'Do not blink.
Stand united, or else sink.'

Elegy for Mandela

He broke the law because it was bad law.
Nelson understood what his life was for:
to confront the rule of the white man's gun.
Now we won't see the likes of him anymore.
He didn't count the cost, but he kept the score.

He didn't care what the enemy had in store.
When breaking rocks in the African sun
he kept his eyes on the long-term prize,
and later forgave them for what they'd done.
We won't see the likes of him anymore.

Most of us don't know what our lives are for.
But Mandela knew what he'd come to do.
He opposed the injustice that he saw
as he believed that change was overdue.
We won't see the likes of him anymore.

We won't see or hear him anymore.
And a nation mourns, for its heart is raw
from the Cape Town Flats to the Great Karoo.
Mandela knew what he had come here for.
And there won't be men like him anymore.

Food for Thought

An Ode to Indecision

If you are prone to indecisiveness
and life just won't make sense,
it's best to stay right where you are,
sitting firmly on the fence.

If you don't know which way to go,
can't choose from left or right;
be glad to know that you don't know
and rise above the fight.

All commitment's fraught with danger!
Strong convictions lead to wars.
So let caution be your watchword.
Do not advance a cause.

Just think of all the bloodshed
caused by those who *know* they're right.
At least half of them must have been wrong
or they could not have had a fight.

They say courage is a virtue.
But what if they are wrong?
What you don't do will not hurt you.
Do not rush to belong.

If someone's trying to enlist you,
hold tight to indecision.
Here are words that will assist you
when confronted by division:

'I need to think it over'
'I'm unconvinced by what you say'
'I struggle with polarities'
'I see only shades of grey'.

And there are short words you can utter
that defer to middle ground -
well...but...mm...er...
or any sort of mumbling sound.

Beware of the impetuous.
They may live to repent
and boldly grasp at indecisiveness
when their convictions are all spent.

If you are asked for a prediction,
then just say 'Wait and see'.
And if they get persistent,
reply 'Oh, don't ask me'.

Take comfort in uncertainty.
It's philosophically quite sound.
It proves that you're a thinker.
Doubt makes the world go round.

Fools may not Speak

Who are the wise men?
Who are the fools?
Who makes things happen?
Who are their tools?
Who dictates fashion?
Who follows on?
Who points the finger
at all that is wrong?

Who's in control
and what do they want?
Who pays the price
for the billionaire's jaunt?
Who dictates the lessons
we teach in our schools
to shape the next wave
of obedient fools?

And where are the wise men?
Do they still exist?
Are they just hiding
or hard to enlist?
Where are we going
and who really cares
if few understand who
decides on the shares?

In a privatised future
the public retreats
to individualised culture
with few cushioned seats;
too tired to ask questions,
too puzzled to think,
all stumbling onward
in a world out of sync.

Lost Costings

Are the things we forget to forget
the same things we don't want to remember?
We don't want to recall them, and yet
it seems we can never dismember
those memories and all that goes with them
that have made us the people we are.
It's apparent we cannot dismiss them.
It's transparent we can't hide the scar.

Whereas what we want to remember
will elude us, more often than not;
like a fire reduced to an ember,
like a narrative without a plot;
like a thought in search of its logic,
an impression of something long lost;
an echo of something so tragic
we can't calculate its true cost.

An Airport

An airport's a peculiar place.
It is a most inhuman space
where people shuffle round in queues,
take off their belts, bracelets and shoes
to be fondled by a stranger's hands
and acquiesce to odd demands.

It is not natural to fly.
And so perhaps that explains why
before we're launched into the cloud
we submit to things that aren't allowed
in other public places where
such goings on are very rare.

We overlook an airport's crimes.
They are a feature of our times;
and so unlike not long ago
when travelling was nice and slow.
Now are we so much better off
by spending so much time aloft?

The Annual Ritual

There's a sense of occasion at the end of December
when we look forward and think of the things we intend:
a time to reflect in the year-ending embers
on what to preserve and what to amend:

a time to take stock as the clocks point to midnight;
a time to resolve and a time to make plans;
a time to project what we'd most like to be like;
a time to look hard at where everyone stands;

a time to take note of another year's passing;
its prizes and sorrows, its highs and its lows;
sentimental impressions, the memories flashing;
sharp as a pin-prick, its joys and its woes;

that time-honoured ritual, how we all adore it.
How else can a year claim its place in the past
and be logged into history, like all those before it,
a time frame completed, recorded to last?

ee cummings

Untypical of his generation,
ee cummings did not do punctuation.
You'll find his verses are unfettered
by the use of any capital letters.

I often wonder what his problem was?
Perhaps cummings wrote like that because
if there's one sure way to get attention
it is by defying word convention.

In other respects he was a decent man.
Yet I feel compelled to say I'm not a fan
as he undermined what is taught in schools;
and there are good reasons for those old rules.

Although cummings left us a long time ago
his predilection still fills me with woe.
What's next? The spaces between the words?
Well, wouldn't that be yet more absurd?

A Limerick to Shakespeare

There once lived a poet near Warwick
whose sonnets were truly a tonic.
He also wrote plays
that today still amaze.
And his legacy? Well, it's iconic.

The Disturbed Poem

Nobody has a right to live life undisturbed.
The suggestion that you do is really quite absurd.
For nothing can stand still, and if you look close enough,
stuff's forever changing into other kinds of stuff.

No man is an island. For if a man's alive
he'll need the help of others in order to survive.
On entering and leaving, we all need that helping hand;
and navigation doesn't work when we lose sight of land.
When we look closely at our borders, the markings become
   blurred.
And that's why no one has a right to live life undisturbed.

You are your brother's keeper. Make an effort, feel his need.
When the dogs of war start baying it's the innocent who
   bleed.
Look beyond your garden, sense what's in the air.
It won't respect your borders. Did you put it there?
Once a thing's created, it journeys undeterred.
And that's another reason why we all should be disturbed.

The woman in the advert offers money unsecured;
she preys on desperation, her victims swiftly lured
into voluntary slavery to serve the lender's venal game.
The game is not illegal, though its rules are quite insane.
Who is that a-laughing? Could it be a mockingbird
observing mankind's folly? So why aren't we disturbed?

Look at that man of business, seduced by all his profit;
a-clinging to the tiger's back, afraid he may fall off it.
With each fibre of his being wrapped around the bottom
  line,
he ignores the far horizon. He hasn't got the time.
So tunnelled is his vision, his ears have never heard
that he doesn't really have the right to live life
  undisturbed.

For he's doing unto others what others do to him;
though he doesn't want to see this. His moral light is dim.
He's a product of a system that he wants to reproduce.
Someone tried to tell him; but it wasn't any use.
There are so many like him who prefer their vision blurred.
There are billions who still believe they can live life
  undisturbed!

When we consider what we vote for, too many now agree
that we allocate allegiance by 'what's in it for me?'.
The barriers are rising, social classes draw apart,
encouraged by the influence of the politician's art.
And so our dormant conscience is reluctant to be stirred;
suffocated by the zeitgeist, it fails to be disturbed.

We know it's all unravelling. We can feel the pressing
  threat.
The direction we've been travelling has burdened us with
  debt.
In debt to Mother Nature; to God, if he exists.
Yet we do not change direction; the policy persists.
Can we encapsulate it? If so, what is the word?
Considering the options, it has to be 'absurd'.

Deep within our heart of hearts there is a sacred place,
where conscience and the way we are behold each other's
    face.
It's not a place of comfort. It strips our motives bare
when we swim beyond the shallows and see what's
    lurking there.
What is going on now? Whose agenda's being served?
Could it be the interests who refuse to be disturbed?

Man is fuelling his crisis by the debts he has incurred.
Can you ask yourself the question, is my integrity
    disturbed?
Can you recognise the problem? Can you see it must be
    curbed?
Can you see that no one has a right to live life undisturbed?

Modern Accessories

*'We live in an age when unnecessary things are our only true
necessities.' Oscar Wilde*

Now the world is obsessed with the latest accessories,
the unnecessary things are the only necessities.

There's no food in his belly, no shoes on his feet,
yet with his latest gadget his life feels complete.
He is dying by trying to keep up with the trend,
to follow the fashions that will fashion his end;
for those mystical moments that twitter his soul,
for the flashing of Facebook that makes him feel whole;
he will sacrifice all that makes living worthwhile -
another voluntary victim of modernity's guile.

I wish I'd had more sex

'Yes, I haven't had enough sex.'
Sir John Betjeman, when asked if he had any regrets.

When we get too old to do it
will we miss what we've not done?
When we sit back and review it
will we wish that we'd begun
to explore the hopes we left unturned
and the ones that got away?
Will we gaze on bridges idly burned
and look back with dismay?

When we get too old to do it
how will we use our time?
When it's gone we can't renew it.
Time becomes a worn out mine
when we know the best's behind us
and what's left is hard to get.
Then will what we've done remind us
not to focus on regret?

On the Dark Side

This Land is My Land
(with apologies to Woody Guthrie)

This land is my land.

   This land is my land.

Take note of what I said
or you'll end up dead.
And stop repeating what I say.
We are in charge.
We will have our way!

   We will have our way.
   We belong and we must stay.
   You must go away.
   The world is on our side.

America's on our side.
You cannot turn the tide.
We will not go away.
We belong. We will stay.

   Now you're repeating my words!
   Your argument's absurd.
   The world hates your guts.

That's as maybe, but…
there are no ifs or buts.
You people are nuts.
And it has been ordained
YOU must be contained.

   Our people have rights.

You're provoking the fights.

That's because we're oppressed.

But we have been blessed.

You've murdered our sons.

We have the most guns.

And you've bombed our schools.

You don't play by the rules
so why should we care?

Because the world has condemned you.

Look, we didn't intend to
murder those kids.
It wasn't OUR fault
what YOUR terrorists did.

They started the trouble
and that is why Gaza's
been bombed into rubble.

We will not give in.

We will not give in.

This land is mine.
I will defend it with a landmine.

To mine the land makes the whole world blind.
That's the message Gandhi left behind.
What you are doing is a crime.

The Bible says an eye for an eye.

Gandhi said that's wrong.

Did he say why?

He said it makes the whole world blind.

But first, we must defend our kind.
I mined the land as the land is mine.
An Arab wouldn't understand
and an Arab cannot make demands.
And you are standing on my land!
The land is mine!

The land is mine.
And the name of it is Palestine!

Oh you can keep your Palestine...
what's left of it.
Now most is mine.
And we will keep Jerusalem.
Amen. Amen. Jerusalem!
And when more settlers come
we'll make room for them.

By taking more of my land.

The land is ours and we have the powers.

This land is my land.

This land is my land.

And as both sides fed each other's fears,
they argued on for years and years
as they watered the Holy Land with their tears.

Frequently Asked Questions

Oh, what is happening in the East?
Explain the grisly scene.
How will it end? Who'll win? Who'll lose?
What does the bad news mean?

Why have they slaughtered innocents
who only tried to help?
  They are slaughtering those innocents
  to make our leaders yelp.

But where does ISIS get its guns?
What horrors they inflict!
  They get their guns from us, and so
  that's how they're well equipped.

  The Iraqi army ran away.
  Their leaders turned and fled.
  That's why we're where we are today.
  And more blood must be shed.

But how come they recruit our young?
Oh, what is their appeal?
  They appeal to those who are possessed
  by suicidal zeal.

  The West is ruled by plutocrats
  who ignore the common good.
  So some look to the theocrats
  to stain our world with blood.

They've observed our crass vulgarities
and don't like what they see.
Now they've chained themselves to a crazy cause
in an effort to be free.

But who will win the war of words?
Whose message will prevail?
  The victor writes his history;
  the loser's left to wail.

But what is it that ISIS wants?
Can't we negotiate?
  You can't cut deals with those whose hearts
  have only room for hate.

But why does ISIS hate us so?
What's made them all so bad?
  Some think it's all the wars they've known
  that have made them all go mad.

  Their lands have long been killing fields;
  a ceaseless desert Somme.
  As fear breeds fear, breeds fear, breeds fear,
  the story carries on.

And who will win out in the end?
Oh, can you tell me that?
  Why those who make the guns of course,
  whose profits have grown fat.

That sounds so sick! It can't be right.
Is that what wars are for?
  Oh, ask the ones who make the guns.
  It's they who know the score.

Holy, Holy, Holy

Holy, holy, holy;
it's an unholy mess.
The rockets of the Israelites
are firing to excess.

Obama says please stop it.
Europe's leaders plead likewise;
although they've banked the profits
from those rockets in the skies.

We've sold our arms to help them
maintain their ways of strife.
Slaughter from the skyways
is stronger than the knife.

Holy, holy, holy;
The Holy Land's on fire.
The Gaza Strip is smitten.
The situation's dire.

The Israelites are angry.
The Hamasites are mad.
The death toll is lopsided.
How many more to add?

We're haunted still by déjà vu.
We have been here before.
We fear there's no solution
to this most ancient war.

Holy, holy, holy;
it's an unholy mess.
Are these God's chosen children
who he's been said to bless?

Hard to Kill

We can shoot them, burn them, bomb them:
we can do all this, yet still
the malignancy grows stronger.
A bad idea's hard to kill.

Their barbarity disgusts us;
makes the civilized feel ill.
We vow we must destroy them, but
a bad idea's hard to kill.

Can't bear to hear the latest news -
we feel we've had our fill.
We know we must confront it, yet
a bad idea's hard to kill.

Our Western ways are under threat –
we fear the mounting bill.
We're sinking into deeper debt, yet
the thing's still hard to kill.

Shoot them! Burn them! Bomb them!
Our generals know the drill.
It feels like we've been here before.
A bad idea is hard to kill.

Their Path Divided

Their path divided as they knew it would.
It wasn't love, but they loved it as such,
until they grew tired of the sight of blood.

In the beginning, passion surged like a flood.
In the end, the effort had become too much.
Then their path divided, as they knew it would.

She was no diva and he was no stud,
yet to be human is to need love's crutch.
It gets harder when it's stained with blood.

Neither admitted, though both understood,
that they had drifted too far out of touch.
So their path divided as they knew it would.

They no longer felt as they knew they should.
Love was a memory beyond their clutch;
both had grown tired of the sight of blood.

Though all love starts life as a tender bud,
once its glory fades, no one can retouch.
Their path divided as they knew it would.
They had both had enough of the sight of blood.

Modern Medication

Woken by her old alarm clock, she reaches for her
medication;
the child-mother-grandparent, member of the modern
nation.
She often wakes up weeping for the kids who never call;
for the secrets long in keeping, for the sadness of it all.

She switches on the wireless, it's company of a kind;
a one-way communication to mask what's on her mind.
Then breakfasted and face on, she's ready for the day;
and paints a cheerful smile on to cover her dismay.

Prepared to do her duties, as all decent people do;
her modern medication will somehow pull her through.
But best of all is bedtime, when she gets to breathe her last;
so grateful it's all over and that the past's all passed.

American Studies

In Hollywood they like the simple lie
so they paint their characters black or white.
It makes commercial sense to personify
the American Way in a righteous light.

Their films celebrate how the West was won
by exercising overwhelming force:
Christ's message fired from the barrel of a gun
paved the yellow brick road of history's course.

Now it's felt that the Western is passé.
The world's moved on, and we've started to doubt
whether the old cowboys still know the way.
They've led us in. But can they lead us out?

The Coming: a dystopian vision

<u>Canto One</u>   Enter the horsemen

Gatekeeper: The horsemen of the apocalypse
                 ride high upon the plain.
                 It's said that they have called before,
                 now they're calling back again.

Lord of Earth: And what is it they want this time?
                 What hastens their return?
Gatekeeper: They're claiming payment for our crime.
                 They want our world to burn.

Lord of Earth: What crime is it they're speaking of?
                 What nonsense do they say?
Gatekeeper: They claim we've turned our back on love.
                 They will not go away.

                 Now tell me, should I let them in
                 or barricade the door?
                 We've tried atoning for our sin,
                 yet they're demanding more.

Lord of Earth: Then let us raise the barricades
                 and let us find our guns.
                 And let us declare a holy war.
                 We must procure the funds.

                 Our history defines success!
                 God's truth's our source of pride!
Gatekeeper: Oh, he won't solve this bloody mess.
                 God's fighting on both sides!

Lord of Earth: That can't be true, for God is ours;
that's what we have been told.
Gatekeeper: Well, perhaps he has misplaced his powers?
He must be rather old.

Nietzsche said that God is dead;
said he died when things got bad.
He said the Devil's here instead.
Lord of Earth: Oh my God, how sad.

Gatekeeper: Look, it's no use saying 'Oh my God'
if God has truly died,
now that the Devil's riding squad
demands to get inside.

Nietzsche said we could all be gods;
or, at least, supermen.
Lord of Earth: Nietzsche was a lunatic.
Don't speak of him again.

Round up the special forces.
Call up the most devoted.
Gatekeeper: The reply I got of course is –
'They already have revolted'.

Yet it's too late for all of that.
You see, in truth, I lied.
Someone left out a welcome mat.
The horsemen are inside!

Oh hear their drummers drumming.
How could we have been so dumb?
So long we feared their coming…
and now, behold…they've come!

<u>Canto Two</u>   The walls are breached

Gatekeeper: Oh Christ, was Christ right after all
              when he warned us to desist?
              He said we're riding for a fall,
              yet we could not resist.

              We carried on the same old way.
              We failed to heed his call.
              And now that impulse to betray
              brings Judgement Day to all!

Horsemen: Incinerate! Incinerate!
              The sinners all must burn.
              That poisoned apple Adam ate
              has led to our return.

              Incinerate! Incinerate!
              Judgement's hour draws near.
              We are the horsemen at the gate.
              Our purpose here is clear!

              Incinerate! Incinerate!
              We'll turn your world to ash.
              You've etched your fate upon your slate.
              Now death must come to pass!

Gatekeeper: The horsemen made their message plain
              as they thundered through the sky.
              They held the key to death's domain
              where the guilty souls must die.

Horsemen: It's well known that God's gifts to man
have sadly been abused.
Now punishment must be the plan
as mankind stands accused

by us, the horsemen of the night
on this dreaded Judgement Day.
So let the sinners all repent
and wallow in dismay!

It's well known that your moneymen
sit high in London's sky,
a-counting up their pots of gold
far from the poor man's cry.

And it's well known that your governments
have held in high esteem
those sinful, sordid, selfish crimes
no penance can redeem.

The plutocrats, the kleptocrats,
the sowers of your grief,
will be cast down to the sewer rats
who scuttle deep beneath

those glossy, glassy, godless towers
wherein the dealers dealt,
playing poker with their venal powers
that caused the Earth to melt.

And most gave succour to those curs
by engaging in their game.
And now's the day of reckoning.
You've got yourselves to blame.

Canto Three   Satan fights back

Gatekeeper: Then war broke out in heaven,
as the Earth became a hell,
while the serpents and the dragon
drank deep from Satan's well.

And St Michael and his angels
felt that they must give in,
for the Devil is a fiendish foe
who is fuelled by his sin.

Then God sent for reinforcements.
The Holy Lamb was called;
who smote the eyes of Satan,
whose victory was forestalled

as the dragon drifted down to Earth
transmuted as the beast
who fed upon the long lost souls
so recently deceased.

Three witches watching in the gloom,
old floozies round a font.
The Lord said he'd save one from doom;
but which witch did he want?

It's hard to tell which witch is which.
They're hard to tell apart.
And once we choose that witch may switch
hers for another's heart.

Redemption is not what they seek.
Each witch is Satan's slave;
each happy in the mortal ditch
which will become her grave.

Was God seduced by Satan
into thinking dark was light?
The battle had been raging
since God created night.

For sure, old Satan loves his tricks;
and tricks must have a code.
He chose the number six six six
to hide the seeds he sowed.

Then the wine of fornication flowed
and many drank full deep.
The wine of fornication flowed,
and the Devil's dew did seep

into the veins, into the hearts,
into the souls of men,
who fornicated furiously –
again, again, again!

Canto Four   The torments are unleashed

Horsemen: Twenty-four elders robed in white
sit in the higher place.
Twenty-four elders robed in white,
each with a golden face.

Twenty-four elders waiting there,
who know well how to wait,
have decreed the waiting time is up
and man must meet his fate.

The seven seals of the sacred scroll
have been unwrapped at last.
Transgressors all must pay the toll
for now the die is cast.

We are the horsemen of the Lord
whose gift you have betrayed.
We've ridden here with one accord:
to ensure your debt is paid.

Behold, the angel of the abyss
is waiting for her prey!
Her word is written on the wind.
Her word is called - DISMAY.

Two hundred million horsemen
prepare to scourge the Earth.
And the multitudes of sinners
may yet regret their birth.

Multitude: Let us protest our innocence.
We know not what we did!
Our leaders are the ones to blame.
We did as we were bid.

Horsemen:

The cathedrals we constructed
pay homage to our God!
Then you have been misinstructed.
For God thinks that it's odd

the way you've misconstrued Him
and used Him for your gain.
Your system's led to ruin.
Soon nothing will remain.

Two hundred million horsemen,
and each with one intent;
that none of you will rest until
God's fury has been spent.

The winds of woe are blowing
as stars fall from the skies.
You'll pay that which is owing
for trading in your lies.

At the seventh angel's signal
God's vengeance will be done;
the apocalypse completed
by the waning of the sun

when the angel of the abyss
devours her earthly prey.
The word is written on the wind.
The word is called - DISMAY.

The Reunion

On reading about the last ever D-Day reunion on 6th June 2014.

I suppose they went there to remember
the horrors they cannot forget.
There is no way to forget them;
like white sentinels, memories are set.

It's the being with others who've been there
that they're looking to take away;
for them what's past is still present,
more present than today.

I suppose there's a grim satisfaction,
a sombre remembrance that death
was somehow or other evaded
while the reaper was holding his breath.

In the fields of perpetual sorrow
the white sentinels stand there forlorn
to remind us of all those tomorrows
cut down like a field of ripe corn.

Singalong Songs

We Deserve a Better Future

When I think about tomorrow and the world that's yet to
   come,
I feel a sense of sorrow for the foolish things we've done.
We've squandered our resources on long journeys to the
   sun
as the system grinds us down.

chorus: We deserve a better future, we deserve a better future,
we deserve a better future, but the system grinds us down.

We are putting up the shutters on the High Streets of the
   land
and looking for price cutters to meet Amazon's demand.
We've built a mad economy that no one understands
as the system grinds us down.

chorus

We are worried that our way of life may not be here to stay.
So we need a new direction soon before we lose our way.
We are dreaming of a deep blue sky but all we see is grey
as the system grinds us down.

chorus

And we cannot say we didn't know because we had been
   warned
as most of our inheritance has already been pawned.
So now we have to face up to the horrors we have
spawned
while the system grinds us down.

The Bad News Blues: how man lost the argument with the management

Oh Lordy Lord, we got the bad news blues.
You gave us the garden and you let us choose.
You played us for suckers. You knew we'd lose.
Now, Lordy Lord, we got the bad news blues.

We read those holy books based on your views;
the Bible and Koran, they both gave us clues.
But you know that we're weak, programmed to abuse.
And Lordy Lord, we got the bad news blues.

Whose fault was it, Lord? We ask you, whose?
When temptation comes, can a man refuse?
Did you set it all up just to amuse?
Well, it's a bad joke, Jehovah, that we can't excuse.

No, don't blame us, Big Man. The mess is your fault.
You coulda stopped us. You coulda called a halt.
Now we're trapped in this over-heated vault.
And Lordy Lord, we got the bad news blues.

Then God spoke up, made his reply:
said *'It ain't my fault that y'all gonna die.*
There were two paths, and you picked the wrong one –
so just carry on singin that old blues song.

You recall the garden and that choice you had?
There were two paths: one good, one bad.
And it was up to you, you made that choice.
That's why I gave you the gift of a voice!

I said have your say, do as you will.
But come Judgement Day, you'll have to foot the bill.
So don't give me no shit, it was down to you.
Don't give me no bull bout what a man's gotta do.'

Aw God, come on, give us another pop.
It's kinda final just to shut up shop.
Aw, come on God, cut us some slack.
We'll promise to change if you take us back.

And what about all the babies, a-waitin to be born?
Would you abandon them, Lord, to a future that's forlorn?
If you don't mind me sayin, that just ain't fair.
Aw, give us a break, Lord, show us that you care!

'Look...back in the garden, y'all saw the signs.
There was nothin pure, not even in those times.
And lookin at both paths by the settin sun,
you thought the one marked 'bad' sounds much more fun.

You thought, heck...heaven's no fun on a Saturday night;
let's boogie down the road that leads outa sight.
Let's play with guns, deal in LSD.
You turned your backs on love, you turned your backs on me.

You developed knowledge, but you're none the wiser.
You used cocaine for your trip advisor.
Now you're askin for mercy? Well, I'm tellin you no!
Think I mentioned before, you reap what you sow.'

And so it was, man's fall came to pass.
The hard truth is that man lacks true class.
Then all mankind rose up as one,
all singin and a-wailin that old blues song.

It was the last blues song that was ever writ.
We all know what it is now; this is it.
So let's all join in to vent our woes.
Don't be churlish now. You know how it goes.

Let's go down singin, all hand in hand.
We asked God's help, he didn't understand.
We asked for mercy and he said 'no'.
Guess that means it's time for us to go.

All together now, one more time;
seems there ain't no redemption for our crime.
Lordy Lord, we got the bad news blues.
(Yeah…and these were the words of man's final muse.)

Anthem of the Nova Scotia Folk Club

I've come to the Nova for many a year
as this is the old folk club that I prefer.
So I keep on coming. I come back for more.
For that is the point of what folk clubs are for.

chorus (with gusto):
And we'll go on forever…
Pay a pound on the door,
Yes, we'll come to the Nova!
We'll come here evermore.

You'd best get here early if you want to perform.
Sing a song with a chorus, you'll go down a storm.
You'll need to sing loudly. They don't have a mic.
They keep it acoustic, as that's what they like.

The Nova's a folk club that gets in your blood.
There are other folk clubs, but they aren't as good.
I have tried some others. I like to get out.
I found one in Fishponds…but they just folk about!

chorus

You don't need deep pockets. It's only a quid.
And if they don't like you they'll keep it well hid.
It's cheap entertainment. You cannot go wrong.
And you could join in with this terrible song.

chorus

It's a very old folk club with lots of old folk
who like singing songs that aren't short of a joke.
They'll join in the chorus if it's not too hard
and listen to poems by a windmilly bard.

chorus

The Nova's kept going by three wise old men
who have organised it since no one knows when.
If you miss a week, they'll forgive what you've done,
and welcome you back as a prodigal son.

chorus

If you haven't been I suggest that you do.
You too could be part of the jolly old crew.
The drinks are not pricey. It's a decent old pub,
and you could fill your face with traditional grub.

Super Callous Banking Bastards

chorus: Super callous banking bastards really are atrocious.
They've taken all our hard-earned cash and spent it. Holy Moses!
The thought of what those bankers do just makes me feel
ferocious
as super callous banking bastards really are atrocious.
Um-diddle-diddle-diddle um-diddle-eye
Um-diddle-diddle-diddle um-diddle-eye

I had been stashing cash away since I was just a lad.
I thought we all should pay our way and being poor is bad.
I put my savings in a bank, believing banks were good.
But now I've realised that banks do not do what they
should!

chorus

I thought banks were respectable as I was quite naïve.
I didn't realise that bankers set out to deceive.
They shift our money round the world until we are in
doubt
who actually controls the dosh that they all slosh about.

chorus

They pay themselves big bonuses for losing lots of cash.
It was the bankers' recklessness that caused the world to
crash.
The trouble is that they don't mind as we have bailed them
out.
There's nothing much that we can do but spread this song
about.

chorus

Thanks firstly to my editor Sally Britton for her heroic work reviewing, organising and publishing this book. Thanks also to Richard Bradley for his proof-reading and valued feedback. And thank you to everyone who has bought my books or attended my events. This has inspired me to sustain my efforts.

I hope you have enjoyed reading this book as much as I enjoyed writing it. Check out my website for events and further information or email me.

www.windmillbard.co.uk
windmillbard@aol.co.uk

Trevor Carter – the Bard of Windmill Hill